DEDICATION

My Little Catholic Bible
is dedicated to the memory of
P.J. Furlong
September 26, 1994 - March 4, 2006

"Let the children come to me;
do not prevent them,
for the kingdom of God
belongs to such as these."
Mark 10:14

Presented to

By

On

My Birth

My name is ______________________________

I was born at ____________ o'clock ____________ M

on ______________________________ Date

at ______________________________ Place

in ______________________________ City, State

Doctor ______________________________

Pediatrician ______________________________

Nurses ______________________________

I weighed __________ lbs. __________ ozs.

and measured ______________________________ inches

My hair was __________ and my eyes were __________

I was named ______________________________

because ______________________________

I was the ______________________________ child

of (Father) ______________________________

and of (Mother) ______________________________

My home was at ______________________________

____

My Baptism

I received the Sacrament of Baptism

on ______________________________ *Date*

at ______________________________ *Church*

in ______________________________ *, Parish*

The Reverend ______________________________

baptized me and my godfather, ______________________________

and my godmother, ______________________________

sponsored me.

These friends and relatives were present:

____

____

____

____

____

____

____

____

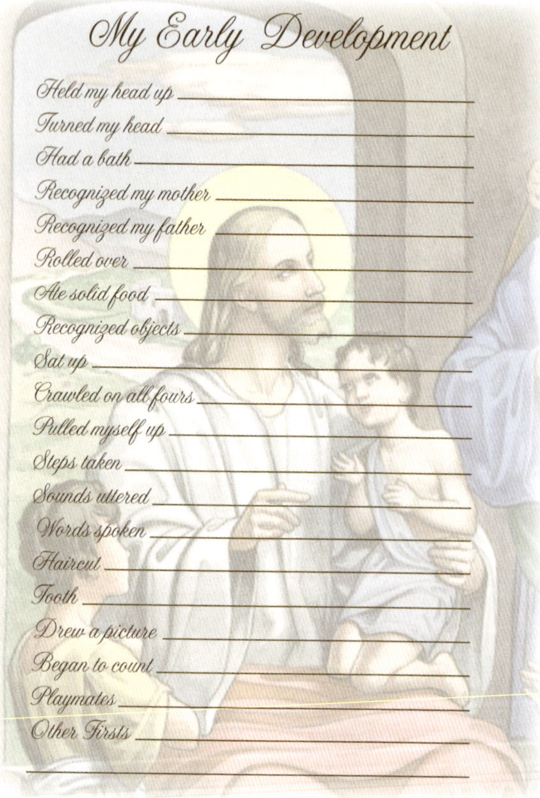

My Early Development

Held my head up ______________________

Turned my head ______________________

Had a bath ______________________

Recognized my mother ______________________

Recognized my father ______________________

Rolled over ______________________

Ate solid food ______________________

Recognized objects ______________________

Sat up ______________________

Crawled on all fours ______________________

Pulled myself up ______________________

Steps taken ______________________

Sounds uttered ______________________

Words spoken ______________________

Haircut ______________________

Tooth ______________________

Drew a picture ______________________

Began to count ______________________

Playmates ______________________

Other Firsts ______________________

____

My Favorite Things

Toys ______________________________

____

Clothes ______________________________

____

Pets ______________________________

____

Games ______________________________

____

Stories ______________________________

____

Prayers ______________________________

____

Songs ______________________________

____

T.V. Show ______________________________

____

Playmates ______________________________

____

____

Other Favorites ______________________________

____

____

Memorable Firsts

My Mother and Father taught me how to pray as a child.
This is the first prayer I ever learned.

____

____

In time, I learned these important prayers.

______________________________ Age ________

______________________________ Age ________

On ____________________ at the age of ________

my Mother and Father brought me to ____________

____________________________________ Church

in ____

On ____________________ at the age of ________

I began my religious education at ______________

____________________________________ School

in ____

I was in ______________ grade and my teacher was

____

I attended my first Mass on __________________

at ___________________________________ Church

in ____

The Reverend ____________________ was the celebrant.

I was __________ years old.

Sacraments I Received

Reconciliation

I received the Sacrament of Reconciliation at the age of

______________ on ________________________

at ________________________________ Church

in ______________________________________

The Reverend ______________ heard my confession.

First Holy Communion

I received Jesus in the Eucharist for the first time on

________________ at ______________ Church.

I was ______________ years old. The Reverend

________________ celebrated the Mass, and the

Reverend ________________ gave me communion.

Confirmation

I became a soldier of Christ on ______________

at ________________________________ Church

in ______________________________________

I was ____________ years old. Bishop ____________

confirmed me and ______________ was my sponsor.

I took the name of ______________ in Confirmation.

My Little Catholic
BIBLE

Edited by

Ruth Hannon

Rev. Victor Hoagland, C.P.

Illustrations by

J. Verleye

Regina Press

www.reginapress.com

Nihil Obstat: Text taken from approved and traditional sources.
Rev. Msgr. Richard Henning, S.T.D.
Censor librorum
July 25, 2011

Imprimatur: Most Reverend William Murphy
Bishop of Rockville Centre
July 26, 2011

THE REGINA PRESS
10 Hub Drive
Melville, New York 11747
www.reginapress.com

Printed in China.

ISBN# 9780882712840
CPSIA January 2013 10 9 8 7 6 5 4 3 2 1 SC

The Old Testament

God Made the World

Genesis 1:1–31, 2:1–25

In the beginning God made the earth and the skies. He gathered the waters of the earth together to make the seas. Then God said, "Let plants and trees grow upon the earth," and it was done. Then God made the sun and the moon, and He filled the sky with stars. He said, "Let the waters and skies be filled with living things, and let animals dwell upon the earth." And it came to pass as God had said.

And God made a man and a woman, and he saw that all he had done was good. In six days God made the world and on the seventh he rested.

Adam and Eve

Genesis 2:1–25, 3:1–24

The Lord God made Adam, the first man, and placed him in the Garden of Eden. God told Adam that he might eat anything in the garden except the fruit of the tree of knowledge. Then God made a woman, Eve, and she was Adam's companion. But a serpent said to Eve, "God forbids you to eat that fruit because if you do, you will become like him." Adam and Eve disobeyed God and ate that fruit.

God knew what they had done, and He said, "Because you have not obeyed me, you must leave this place." So Adam and Eve went out sadly from the beautiful Garden of Eden.

Noah's Ark

Genesis 6:1–22, 7:1–23, 8:1–22

In time, people grew so wicked that God said to Noah, "I shall send a flood, but you will be saved because you are a good man. Build an ark and take into it your family and two of every kind of animal." Noah did as God commanded.

Then the rains fell for forty days and destroyed all living things except Noah and the others in the ark. After the storm was over, Noah set a dove free. When it did not return, Noah knew it had found a place to perch and that the waters had gone down. Then he and the others stepped forth on dry land.

God Calls Abram

Genesis 12:1–9, 15:1–21, 17:1–22, 21:1–8

The Lord said to Abram, "Leave your home and go to a land I will show you." So Abram went out of his house with Sarai, his wife, and all he owned. When he came to Canaan, the Lord said, "I will give this land to you and to your family forever." And Abram and Sarai dwelt in Canaan.

The Lord was pleased with Abram, and He said to him, "Your name will now be Abraham, and your wife's will be Sarah. I will give you a son whom you will call Isaac." When the obedient Abraham and Sarah had a son, they named him Isaac, as the Lord had commanded.

Jacob's Vision

Genesis 25:19–26 (Birth), 28:10–26 (Dream)

Abraham's son, Isaac, was the father of Jacob. One night when Jacob was on a journey, he lay on the ground and slept. In a dream he saw a ladder that reached to heaven, and on it angels were going up and down. Then the Lord said to Jacob, "I am the God of Abraham and of Isaac. I will give you and your children the land on which you are lying, and in your family the earth will be blessed."

When Jacob woke up, he said, "The Lord was here! This is the house of God and the gate of heaven." And he called that place Bethel.

Joseph and His Brothers

Genesis 37:1–36

Jacob had many sons, but Joseph was the one he loved best. When Jacob made Joseph a fine coat, his brothers grew angry and planned to kill the boy. But they decided to sell him instead. After they took away his coat, they sold him to some traders for twenty pieces of silver.

Then the brothers dipped the coat into animal blood and sent it to Jacob, their father. The old man cried, "This is the coat of my son. He has been killed by wild beasts."

But Joseph was alive, for the traders had sold him as a slave in the land of Egypt.

Joseph In Egypt

Genesis 41:1–46

While Joseph was a slave in Egypt, Pharaoh, the King, sent for him and said, "I dreamt I saw seven fat cows, but seven thin cows ate them up. Then I saw seven fine ears of wheat, but seven thin ears swallowed them. What is the meaning of this dream?"

Joseph said, "God will send seven good years and then seven years when nothing will grow. In the good years let a wise man store food for people to eat in the bad years."

"You are wise, Joseph," said Pharaoh, "and I place this land in your care." He gave Joseph a ring, and people bowed down to him.

Joseph Saves His Family

Genesis 42:1–38, 44:1–34, 45:1–28, 46:1–34, 47:1–12

Joseph had enough wheat to feed all of Egypt in the bad years. But at home, his father, Jacob, had no food. He told his sons, "Go down to Egypt for wheat." When Joseph saw his brothers, he knew them at once, but none of them knew him.

They told him about their young brother, Benjamin, whom their father loved, and about Joseph who they said had died.

Then Joseph said, "I am your brother, and I forgive you for selling me to strangers. Bring my father to Egypt to live." Jacob and his sons went to Egypt, and there they made their homes.

The Baby Moses

Exodus 2:1–10

In Egypt, Pharaoh ordered that all Israelite boy babies be killed. Now a certain Israelite woman had a son. To save him, she put him in a basket which she hid by the river while his sister kept watch nearby.

When Pharaoh's daughter, a princess, came to the river, she picked up the baby and cried, "An Israelite child!" The baby's sister asked, "Shall I get an Israelite woman to nurse him?" "Yes," said the princess, and the girl fetched her mother who cared for the baby until he grew up. Then she took him to the princess who named him Moses.

The Burning Bush

Exodus 3:1–22, 4:10–31

While Moses guarded his sheep one day, he saw a bush that was on fire. He went up to it and heard the Lord calling, "Moses!" Moses said, "Here I am." "Take your sandals from your feet," said the Lord," you are on holy ground." And the Lord said, "Moses, I know how cruelly Pharaoh treats the Israelites. Tell him you will lead them out of Egypt."

"But I do not speak well," said Moses. "How can I talk to Pharaoh?" Your brother Aaron is a good speaker," said the Lord. "Take him to Pharaoh, and I shall tell him what to say." Moses did as the Lord commanded.

Moses and Aaron See Pharaoh

Exodus 5:1–5, 7:1–13

Moses went with his brother, Aaron, to Pharaoh and said, "The Lord commands you to let the Israelites go." But Pharaoh said, "No! They must stay here." The Lord then commanded Aaron to cast down his staff before Pharaoh. When he obeyed, the staff became a snake.

Pharaoh then commanded his wise men to do as Aaron had done, and each of their staffs also turned into a snake. But Aaron's staff swallowed all the others. Still Pharaoh would not let the Israelites go. But Moses knew the Lord would save his people.

Across the Red Sea

Exodus 12:31–39, 13:17–22, 14:5–28

At last Pharaoh let the Israelites go, and Moses led them to the Red Sea. But Pharaoh changed his mind and sent his soldiers to bring the Israelites back. The people were frightened when they saw the soldiers, but God said to Moses, "Lift your staff over the sea. It will open and the people may walk across on dry land."

Moses obeyed and the people marched to the other shore. But the soldiers followed them into the passage, and the Lord told Moses, "Stretch your staff over the sea again." The waters closed over the soldiers and all were drowned.

IV
V
VI
VII
VIII
IX

The Commandments

Exodus 19:1–2, 16–25, 29:1–17, 24:12–18

When the Israelites came to the desert of Sinai, they saw a mountain covered with clouds. From its top a trumpet sounded loudly. Moses told the people to wait while he went up the mountain, and there the Lord told him how he expected his people to act. They were to tell the truth. They were to love God and honor their parents. They were to say God's name respectfully. They were not to steal or to hurt others. These were God's Commandments.

The Lord wrote his Commandments on two stone tablets and gave them to Moses to carry down to the people.

The Golden Calf

Exodus 32:1–20, 30–35, 34:1–34

When Moses came down from the mountain, he saw the people dancing around a calf made of gold and worshiping it as their true God. This made Moses so angry that he threw down the stone tablets and broke them. "You have offended God," he cried, and he destroyed the golden calf.

Again Moses went up the mountain, and again God gave him stone tablets upon which He wrote the Commandments. Moses stayed on Mount Sinai for forth days, talking with the Lord. When he came down, his face shone so brightly that he had to cover it with a veil.

The Walls of Jericho

Joshua 1:1–9, 6:1–21

After Moses died, Joshua led the Israelites toward Jericho in Canaan. But a wall had been build around this city to keep the Israelites out. Then the Lord said to Joshua, "Let the people march around Jericho once a day for six days. On the seventh day, let them march seven times. Then, when the priests blow on rams' horns, let all the people shout."

Joshua obeyed, and on the last day when the people marched around the city, the horns blew and everyone shouted. At once, the walls fell and the Israelites marched into the city, as God had promised.

J. Verleye

Young David

1 Samuel 16:1–11

The Lord said to Samuel, a prophet in Israel, "Go to Jesse in Bethlehem, for I have chosen a king from among his sons. I will show you which one it is. Bless that boy with oil, and one day he will rule my people. Samuel looked at seven sons of Isai, but the Lord said, "It is none of these." Samuel asked Jesse, "Are these all the sons you have?" "No," said Isai, "my youngest is minding sheep." Samuel said, "Bring him to me," and this boy was named David. The Lord said to Samuel, "David will be king. Bless him." And God was with David from that day.

David and Goliath

1 Samuel 17:12–54

One morning David took food to his brothers who were in camp. There he heard about Goliath, an enemy soldier who each day called to the Israelites, "Send a man to fight me." But the Israelites were afraid because Goliath was a giant. David said, "I will fight him and God will be with me." Carrying only a sling and five stones, he walked toward the enemy.

Goliath saw David and he ran at him, but the boy threw one of his stones, and it struck Goliath in the forehead. When the giant fell, the enemy soldiers ran away, and the Israelites won the day.

Elijah Is Fed by an Angel

1 Kings 19:1–18

Elijah was a good and holy man, but because he was so good, a wicked queen wanted to harm him. Elijah had to run away.

After he had walked many days and fallen asleep under a tree, an angel came and said, "Get up and eat." Elijah saw bread and a jar of water at his side. He ate and drank and fell asleep again. But once more, the angel came and said, "Get up and eat and drink, for you have a long way to go." Again, Elijah ate and drank. The food was so good that Elijah was able to walk for forty days without eating again.

Personal Record

Name ____________________

Born __________ in ____________________

Baptism

Date ____________________

Priest ____________________

Parish ____________________

Godfather ____________________

Godmother ____________________

First Communion

Date ____________________

Priest ____________________

Parish ____________________

Confirmation

Date ____________________

Bishop ____________________

Parish ____________________

Sponsor ____________________

Confirmation Name ____________________

Family Record

Father ____________________

Born ____________ in ____________

Mother ____________________

Born ____________ in ____________

Brothers and Sisters ____________________

____

____

Father's Family

Grandfather ____________________

Born ____________________

Grandmother ____________________

Born ____________________

Mother's Family

Grandfather ____________________

Born ____________________

Grandmother ____________________

Born ____________________

The New Testament

An Angel Speaks to Mary

Matthew 1:18–25, Luke 1:26–38

In Nazareth there lived a young woman named Mary, who was engaged to Joseph, a carpenter. An angel of the Lord came to her with a message. "Do not be afraid, Mary," said the angel. "God has sent me to tell you that you will be the mother of a son, and his name will be Jesus."

Mary was surprised, but the angel said, "The Holy Spirit will come to you, and your child shall be called the Son of God. He shall rule a kingdom that will last forever."

Mary said, "I am God's servant. I will do what He asks." And the angel went away.

Jesus Is Born

Luke 2:1–20

In time Mary and Joseph, her husband, went to Bethlehem, but the town was crowded and they had to sleep in a cave. Mary's baby, Jesus, was born there that night.

Nearby an angel came to some shepherds who were watching their sheep, and he said "A child has been born in Bethlehem. He is Christ the Lord." And many angels sang:

"Glory to God in the highest,
and peace on earth."

The shepherds went to Bethlehem to see the child, and they found him with Mary and Joseph. Then the shepherds went away praising God.

The Child Jesus in the Temple

Luke 2:41–52

After a holiday, Mary and Joseph were returning home to Nazareth with their friends and the twelve-year-old Jesus. At first Mary thought Jesus was with another family, but when she learned he was not, she and Joseph went back to Jerusalem to look for him. They searched for three days before they found him in a temple. He was talking with teachers who were amazed at his knowledge of God's teachings.

Mary asked, "Son, why have you worried us so?" Jesus answered, "Didn't you know that I must do my Father's work?" But he went home with Mary and Joseph and obeyed them.

The First Apostles

Matthew 4:12–22

When Jesus was thirty years old, he set out to tell people about God's great love for them. One day, as he walked near the Sea of Galilee, he saw two brothers, Peter and Andrew. They were fishing with nets, but Jesus said to them, "Follow me." At once they left their work and went with him.

Further on he saw two other brothers, James and John, who were sitting in a boat with their father mending nets. Jesus asked the brothers to follow him, and they, too, left their work and their father to follow Jesus.

A Marriage at Cana

John 2:1–12

When a marriage was held at Cana, Jesus was there with Mary, his mother. Soon all the wine was gone, and Mary said to Jesus, "There is no wine left." And Jesus asked, "What can I do about it?" But Mary whispered to the waiters, "Do whatever my son commands you." Then Jesus told them, "Fill the tall jars with water and let the headwaiter taste it."

The water had turned into wine, and after the headwaiter took a sip, he said, "It is the best wine we have served today." This was the first of many wonderful things Jesus did.

Jesus Speaks to the People

Matthew 5:1–12; 6:5–15 Luke 6:17–26; 11:1–5

One day Jesus went to a mountain top and spoke to the people. He said, "Love everyone, even those who are not kind to you. Treat others as you want them to treat you, and ask God your Father for whatever you need. Here is how you are to pray to Him:

Our Father who art in heaven, hallowed be thy name. Thy kingdom come, thy will be done on earth as it is in heaven. Give us this day our daily bread, and forgive us our trespasses, as we forgive those who trespass against us. And lead us not into temptation, but deliver us from evil."

A Storm on the Lake

Matthew 8:23–27, Mark 4:35–41, Luke 8:22–25

One evening Jesus said to his apostles, "Let us sail to the other side of the lake." When their boat was out on the water, a storm arose. Winds blew and waves beat against the sides of the little vessel. But Jesus had fallen asleep.

The apostles woke him and cried, "Master, save us or we shall drown!" Jesus stood and said to the sea, "Peace. Be still." At once the winds fell and the sea grew calm. Then Jesus asked the apostles, "Why were you afraid?" And they said to one another, "Who is this Jesus? Even the wind and the waves obey him."

Jesus Feeds the People

Matthew 14:13–21, Mark 6:34–44, Luke 9:10–17, John 6:1–15

A crowd had followed Jesus all day, and in the evening the apostles said, "The people are hungry." The apostle, Philip, announced that a boy had five loaves of bread and two fishes, but that was not enough for so many. Jesus said, "Let the people sit down." After five thousand were seated on the grass, Jesus blessed the loaves and fishes, and the apostles handed them to the crowd. When everyone had eaten, they picked up what was left, and the food filled twelve baskets. The people were amazed that Jesus had fed so many with so little food.

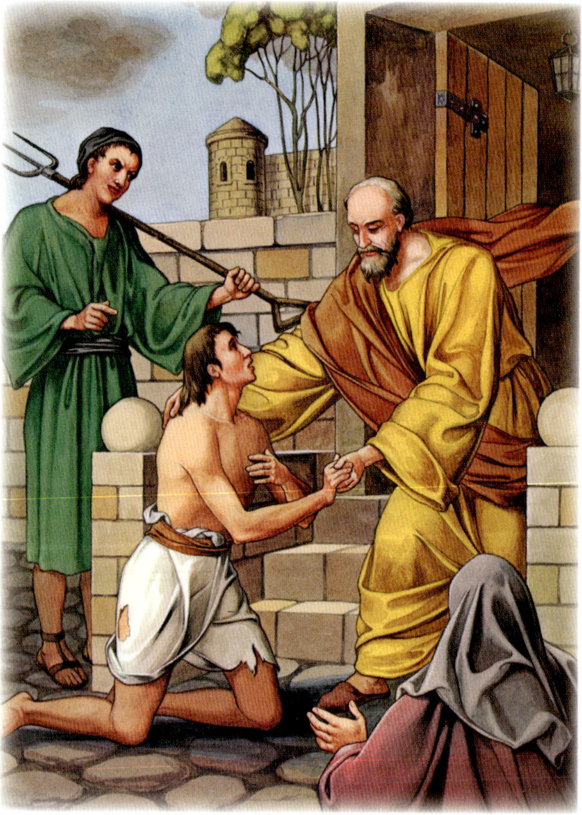

The Loving Father

Luke 15:11–32

A young man left home and went to live in a far place where he spent his money foolishly. When it was all gone, he took a job caring for pigs, but the pigs had more to eat than he had. He said, "The men who work for my father always have enough food. I will go home and ask if I can work for him." He walked along and when his father saw him, he ran to the son and kissed him. And the son said, "Father, I am not worthy to be your son." But the father said to a servant, "Prepare a feast so that we may celebrate my son's return home."

The Story of Zacchaeus

Luke 19:1–10

A rich man named Zacchaeus stood in a crowd that waited to see Jesus.

No one liked Zacchaeus because he made money by collecting taxes from the poor. Because he was short and tall men stood in front of him, he could not see Jesus, so he climbed to a high place. But Jesus called to him, "Come down. I want to stay in your house today." The people said, Why is Jesus going to stay with this wicked man?" But Zacchaeus was sorry for what he had done, and he said, "If I have cheated anyone, I will pay it back," and Jesus was pleased with him.

Jesus Cures a Blind Man

John 9:1–41

When Jesus saw a blind man begging at the side of a road, he put clay on the blind man's eyes and told him to go and wash it off. The man obeyed and at once he was able to see. His parents were amazed, for they knew their son had been born blind and had been that way all his life.

Not long after, Jesus again met the man who had been born blind and asked him, "Do you believe in the Son of God?" The man said, "Who is he? Tell me and I will believe in him." Jesus said, "It is I. You are looking at God's Son." And the man knelt down and worshiped him.

The Raising of Lazarus

John 11:1–44

When Jesus heard that his friend Lazarus had died, he went to visit the dead man's sisters. One of them, Mary, said to Jesus, "If you had been here, Lazarus would not have died."

Jesus said, "Let us go to the cave where he is buried." When they reached it, Jesus said, "Take away the stone that closes the cave." Then he prayed, "Father in heaven, do what I ask you today so that those who are standing here will know it was you who sent me." They he cried, "Lazarus, come out of the tomb." At once the man who had been dead got up and walked out to his friends.

Jesus Enters Jerusalem

Matthew 21:1–11, Mark 11:1–11, Luke 19:28–38, John 12:12–19

When Jesus was near Jerusalem, two of his friends brought him a young ass, and Jesus sat upon it to ride into the city. Many people threw their coats on the road in front of him, and others cut branches from trees and cast them in his path to show their love for Jesus. Those who marched before him began to praise God for the wonderful things Jesus had done for them and for all he had taught them.

They shouted:
"Blessed is he who comes as king in the name of the Lord! Hosanna to the son of David! Glory in the highest."

The Last Supper

Matthew 26:17–30, Mark 14:12–26, Luke 22:14–20

On Holy Thursday, Jesus washed the feet of his apostles and then sat down to eat supper with them. During the meal, he took bread and gave it to the apostles and said, "Take this and eat; it is my body." They he took a cup of wine and said, "Drink this; it is my blood."

And he said to his apostles, "Love one another as I love you. Soon I will leave you to go to my Father. But I will send the Holy Spirit, who will live with you and teach you what you need to know."

Then Jesus and the apostles sang a hymn and prayed together.

Jesus Is Put to Death

Matthew 26:1–75, 27:1–66, Mark 14:1–72, 15:1–47,
Luke 22:1–71, 23:1–56, John 18:1–40, 19:1–42

Men in power hated Jesus because he had said he was the Son of God. Now Judas, one of the apostles, did an evil act. He told the enemies of Jesus where to find him, and on Holy Thursday they arrested him. When the judges asked him if he were truly the Son of God, Jesus would not deny it. They he was flogged, and soldiers put a crown of thorns on his head because the people had called him their king.

On Good Friday, Jesus was taken to Golgotha and nailed to a cross, and there he died. His friends took down his body, wrapped it in a sheet, and buried it in a cave.

The First Easter

Matthew 28:1–10, Mark 16:1–11, Luke 24:1–12, John 20:1–18

On Easter morning, some women went to the tomb where Jesus lay to put spices on his body. Suddenly they remembered that a heavy stone had been rolled in front of the tomb. One woman said, "Who will roll away the stone for us?" But when they got there, it had already been rolled away, and a man in white robes was sitting in the tomb. He said, "Do not be afraid. Jesus has risen from the dead. Tell Peter and the other apostles." As the women ran off, they saw Jesus and knelt to adore him. Jesus said, "Tell the apostles to wait for me in Galilee."

The Apostles See the Risen Jesus

Matthew 28:16–20, Mark 16:12–18, Luke 24:36–49, John 20:19–31

The apostles were indoors when Jesus came to them and said, "Peace be with you." He showed them his wounded hands. But one of the apostles, Thomas, was not there. When the apostles told him they had seen Jesus, he said, "I do not believe it. If I can put my fingers in his wounds, I will believe he is risen."

Again Jesus came, and when he saw Thomas he said, "Put your fingers into my wounds." But Thomas said, "My Lord and my God." Jesus said, "You believe because you see me. Blessed are people who do not see me and who believe."

The Ascension

Mark 16:19–20, Luke 24:50–53, Acts 1:6–12

After Jesus rose from the dead, he stayed on earth for forty days, visiting his apostles and talking to them. He said to them, "Go and teach all people what I have taught you. But wait in Jerusalem until I send you the Holy Spirit." After that, Jesus led them to Mount Olivet and blessed them. Then he rose slowly toward the sky until a cloud hid him from sight. As they kept looking up, two men in white appeared and said, "Men of Galilee, why do you stand gazing up at the sky? Jesus, who has gone to heaven, will return again."

And the apostles went back to Jerusalem.

The Coming of the Holy Spirit

Acts 2:1–13

The apostles, Mary, the mother of Jesus, and their friends prayed and waited for the coming of the Holy Spirit. Then, one day they heard a sound like the wind, and tongues of fire settled on them. All were filled with the Holy Spirit, and they began to speak in many languages. Now visitors from other lands were in Jerusalem, and when the apostles began to speak, the visitors said, "How is it that, no matter what countries we come from, we hear the apostles speaking in our own languages?" The apostles told the story of God's son, and great numbers believed in Jesus and became his followers.